W0038254

THE ROYAL HORTICULTURAL SOCIETY

WILD IN THE GARDEN

DIARY 2021

First published in 2020 by Frances Lincoln Publishing,
an imprint of The Quarto Group.
The Old Brewery, 6 Blundell Street
London, N7 9BH,
United Kingdom
T (0)20 7700 6700
www.QuartoKnows.com

© 2020 Quarto Publishing plc
Photographs © as listed in Picture Credits
Text © 2020 the Royal Horticultural Society and printed
under license granted by the Royal Horticultural Society,
registered charity number 222879/SC038262. An interest
in gardening is all you need to enjoy being a member of
the RHS. Website: rhs.org.uk

Astronomical information © Crown Copyright
Reproduced by permission of HMNAO, UKHO and the
Controller of Her Majesty's Stationary Office.

The Royal Horticultural Society has asserted its moral
right to be identified as the Author of this Work in
accordance with the Copyright Designs and Patents Act
1988.

All rights reserved. No part of this book may be
reproduced or utilised in any form or by any means,
electronic or mechanical, including photocopying,
recording or by any information storage and retrieval
system, without permission in writing from Frances
Lincoln Publishing.

Every effort has been made to trace the copyright holders
of material quoted in this book. If application is made in
writing to the publisher, any omissions will be included in
future editions.

A catalogue record for this book is available from the
British Library.

ISBN 978 0 7112 4733 8

10 9 8 7 6 5 4 3 2 1

Design by Sarah Pyke

Printed in China

RHS FLOWER SHOWS 2021

The Royal Horticultural Society holds a number of
prestigious flower shows throughout the year. At the
time of going to press, show dates for 2021 had not been
confirmed but details can be found on the website at:
rhs.org.uk/shows-events

Every effort is made to ensure calendrical data is correct
at the time of going to press but the publisher cannot
accept any liability for any errors or changes.

PICTURE CREDITS

All photographs are from Shutterstock © **Maxim
Denissenko** Front cover; **Helen J Davies** Back cover, Week
28, Week 43; **Rudmer Zwerver** Title page; **Hannamariah**
Introduction; **Erni** Week 2; **Maciej Olszewski** Week 3;
Ainars Aunins Week 4; **Wojciech Skora** Week 5; **Jack53**
Week 7; **Giedriius** Week 8, Week 39; **iSpb** Week 9; **Ian_
Sherriffs** Week 11; **Eileen Kumpf** Week 12; **Curioso** Week
13; **Jamie Hall** Week 14, Week 21; **Belizar** Week 16; **Erni**
Week 17; **Andrew E Gardner** Week 19, Week 35; **Bunsview**
Week 20; **J K Daylight** Week 22 ; **Ioana Rut** Week 24; **Steve
Midgley** Week 25; **Tgladkova** Week 26; **Venars.original**
Week 29; **Rebecca McCree** Week 30; **Linda George** Week
31; **Hxdbzxy** Week 33; **Chris Moody** Week 34, Week 41;
Mark Caunt Week 37; **Pictoplay** Week 38; **Radovan Zierik**
Week 42; **Rosalind Kirk** Week 44; **Christopher P McLeod**
Week 46; **Florian Teodor** Week 47; **Muddy Knees** Week 48;
Rose-Marie Henriksson Week 50; **AllanW** Week 51; **Kzww**
Week 52; **Daniel Jack Lee** Week 1.

MIX
Paper from
responsible sources
FSC® C008047

CALENDAR 2021

JANUARY

M	T	W	T	F	S	S
				1	2	3
4	5	6	7	8	9	10
11	12	13	14	15	16	17
18	19	20	21	22	23	24
25	26	27	28	29	30	31

FEBRUARY

M	T	W	T	F	S	S
1	2	3	4	5	6	7
8	9	10	11	12	13	14
15	16	17	18	19	20	21
22	23	24	25	26	27	28

MARCH

M	T	W	T	F	S	S
1	2	3	4	5	6	7
8	9	10	11	12	13	14
15	16	17	18	19	20	21
22	23	24	25	26	27	28
29	30	31				

APRIL

M	T	W	T	F	S	S
			1	2	3	4
5	6	7	8	9	10	11
12	13	14	15	16	17	18
19	20	21	22	23	24	25
26	27	28	29	30		

MAY

M	T	W	T	F	S	S
					1	2
3	4	5	6	7	8	9
10	11	12	13	14	15	16
17	18	19	20	21	22	23
24	25	26	27	28	29	30
31						

JUNE

M	T	W	T	F	S	S
	1	2	3	4	5	6
7	8	9	10	11	12	13
14	15	16	17	18	19	20
21	22	23	24	25	26	27
28	29	30				

JULY

M	T	W	T	F	S	S
			1	2	3	4
5	6	7	8	9	10	11
12	13	14	15	16	17	18
19	20	21	22	23	24	25
26	27	28	29	30	31	

AUGUST

M	T	W	T	F	S	S
						1
2	3	4	5	6	7	8
9	10	11	12	13	14	15
16	17	18	19	20	21	22
23	24	25	26	27	28	29
30	31					

SEPTEMBER

M	T	W	T	F	S	S
		1	2	3	4	5
6	7	8	9	10	11	12
13	14	15	16	17	18	19
20	21	22	23	24	25	26
27	28	29	30			

OCTOBER

M	T	W	T	F	S	S
				1	2	3
4	5	6	7	8	9	10
11	12	13	14	15	16	17
18	19	20	21	22	23	24
25	26	27	28	29	30	31

NOVEMBER

M	T	W	T	F	S	S
1	2	3	4	5	6	7
8	9	10	11	12	13	14
15	16	17	18	19	20	21
22	23	24	25	26	27	28
29	30					

DECEMBER

M	T	W	T	F	S	S
		1	2	3	4	5
6	7	8	9	10	11	12
13	14	15	16	17	18	19
20	21	22	23	24	25	26
27	28	29	30	31		

CALENDAR 2022

JANUARY

M	T	W	T	F	S	S
					1	2
3	4	5	6	7	8	9
10	11	12	13	14	15	16
17	18	19	20	21	22	23
24	25	26	27	28	29	30
31						

FEBRUARY

M	T	W	T	F	S	S
	1	2	3	4	5	6
7	8	9	10	11	12	13
14	15	16	17	18	19	20
21	22	23	24	25	26	27
28						

MARCH

M	T	W	T	F	S	S
	1	2	3	4	5	6
7	8	9	10	11	12	13
14	15	16	17	18	19	20
21	22	23	24	25	26	27
28	29	30	31			

APRIL

M	T	W	T	F	S	S
				1	2	3
4	5	6	7	8	9	10
11	12	13	14	15	16	17
18	19	20	21	22	23	24
25	26	27	28	29	30	

MAY

M	T	W	T	F	S	S
						1
2	3	4	5	6	7	8
9	10	11	12	13	14	15
16	17	18	19	20	21	22
23	24	25	26	27	28	29
30	31					

JUNE

M	T	W	T	F	S	S
		1	2	3	4	5
6	7	8	9	10	11	12
13	14	15	16	17	18	19
20	21	22	23	24	25	26
27	28	29	30			

JULY

M	T	W	T	F	S	S
				1	2	3
4	5	6	7	8	9	10
11	12	13	14	15	16	17
18	19	20	21	22	23	24
25	26	27	28	29	30	31

AUGUST

M	T	W	T	F	S	S
1	2	3	4	5	6	7
8	9	10	11	12	13	14
15	16	17	18	19	20	21
22	23	24	25	26	27	28
29	30	31				

SEPTEMBER

M	T	W	T	F	S	S
			1	2	3	4
5	6	7	8	9	10	11
12	13	14	15	16	17	18
19	20	21	22	23	24	25
26	27	28	29	30		

OCTOBER

M	T	W	T	F	S	S
					1	2
3	4	5	6	7	8	9
10	11	12	13	14	15	16
17	18	19	20	21	22	23
24	25	26	27	28	29	30
31						

NOVEMBER

M	T	W	T	F	S	S
	1	2	3	4	5	6
7	8	9	10	11	12	13
14	15	16	17	18	19	20
21	22	23	24	25	26	27
28	29	30				

DECEMBER

M	T	W	T	F	S	S
			1	2	3	4
5	6	7	8	9	10	11
12	13	14	15	16	17	18
19	20	21	22	23	24	25
26	27	28	29	30	31	

GARDENS AND WILDLIFE

Gardens as a network form an important ecosystem. An ecosystem is an interdependent and dynamic system of living organisms which is considered together with the physical and geographical environment. Ecosystems are interdependent because everything in a garden depends on everything else.

The garden ecosystem is extremely variable, thereby offering year-round interest. Gardens offer a large number of animals the perfect conditions for different stages of their life cycle. Insects may prefer sunny, sheltered spots to forage and mate, but their larvae may need to live in water or in rotting vegetation. The large range of garden wildlife is there because of gardening, not despite it.

Due to the nature of gardens, groups of species that exploit a network of gardens' resources can find abundance over a longer time period, compared to what a single natural site can offer. Even gardens that are managed without regard for wildlife still offer some benefit, especially when they are considered as part of the total garden network. Even without simulated 'wild' habitats, gardens are living, diverse ecosystems in their own right. No garden is too small to provide some benefit to wildlife. Many visiting animals can actually be residents of neighbouring gardens. It is the garden network that is of overall importance to wildlife, forming the larger garden ecosystem.

City gardens are important corridors that facilitate the safe movement of birds, butterflies and other wildlife. Wildlife-friendly gardens don't need to be messy, with an abundance of stinging nettles. All gardens offer some resource to certain species, however, with a little thought and planning, every garden can be of great benefit to a much wider range of species. Look around your local area and see what type of habitat is missing and whether it is possible for you to provide it: perhaps a pond, nest-boxes, decaying wood or an undisturbed leaf pile? The more diverse the habitats, the greater the variety of birds and wildlife visiting your garden.

The RHS recognises and actively promotes the valuable contribution that gardens make to wildlife, believing that with thoughtful management it is possible to enhance the wildlife potential in any garden without compromising the gardener's enjoyment of it. For more information visit: www.rhs.org.uk and www.wildaboutgardens.org.uk

'By this time in winter many natural sources of seeds and berries are exhausted, therefore feeding garden birds becomes even more important.'

JOBS FOR THE MONTH
- Hang bird feeders and scatter food on the ground and bird table.
- Good hygiene is essential to prevent diseases so clean the bird bath regularly.
- Check that the water in the bird bath is topped up and not frozen.
- Make sure that the pond does not freeze over.

HEDGEHOGS
During mild spells, hedgehogs can emerge from hibernation for a quick food foray before returning to their hiding places as the temperature drops. They will appreciate having some food left out for them. Hedgehog food is now available but dog food is a good alternative. Bread and milk are not suitable.

IN THE GARDEN
You may want to identify a suitable place in your garden to leave untouched as a wildlife area. Leaves and flower seed-heads can provide winter shelter for ladybirds and other insects. Even a small untended patch behind a shed will be beneficial.

BIRDS
- Blackbirds, thrushes, tits and robins will be visiting the garden.
- **Food:** By this time in winter many natural sources of seeds and berries are exhausted, therefore feeding garden birds becomes even more important.
- Specialist bird food suppliers sell live mealworms, bird seed and fat balls to provide much-needed fat and protein.
- Don't rush to clear windfalls and rotten fruits from the ground, as these provide food for blackbirds, song thrushes and fieldfares.
- Try to keep your feeding regime as consistent as possible so that birds return to the garden.
- **Water:** Regardless of the weather, a regular source of unfrozen water is essential for drinking and bathing so keep containers topped up and ice-free. Periodically scrub out bird baths using specialist detergent (available from bird food suppliers). Always wear suitable protective clothing used especially for these tasks.

WEEK 1

DECEMBER & JANUARY 2021

Monday 28

Tuesday 29

Full moon

Wednesday 30

New Year's Eve

Thursday 31

New Year's Day
Holiday, UK, Republic of Ireland,
USA, Canada, Australia and New Zealand

Friday 1

Saturday 2

Sunday 3

JANUARY

---

4 *Monday*   Holiday, Scotland and New Zealand

---

5 *Tuesday*

---

6 *Wednesday*   Last quarter
                                                                      Epiphany

---

7 *Thursday*

---

8 *Friday*

---

9 *Saturday*

---

10 *Sunday*

European hedgehog *(Erinaceus europaeus)*

JANUARY

Monday **11**

Tuesday **12**

New moon

Wednesday **13**

Thursday **14**

Friday **15**

Saturday **16**

Sunday **17**

Blackbird *(Turdus merula)*

JANUARY

18 *Monday*   Holiday, USA (Martin Luther King Jnr Day)

19 *Tuesday*

20 *Wednesday*   *First quarter*

21 *Thursday*

22 *Friday*

23 *Saturday*

24 *Sunday*

Long tailed tit *(Aegithalos caudatus)*

JANUARY

Monday 25

Holiday, Australia (Australia Day)

Tuesday 26

Wednesday 27

Full moon

Thursday 28

Friday 29

Saturday 30

Sunday 31

Garden spider *(Araneus diadematus)*

FEBRUARY

1 *Monday*

2 *Tuesday*

3 *Wednesday*

4 *Thursday*   *Last quarter*

5 *Friday*

6 *Saturday*   Accession of Queen Elizabeth II
                                                           Waitangi Day (New Zealand)

7 *Sunday*

'Hedges provide important corridors for wildlife to move along safely.'

JOBS FOR THE MONTH
- Put up nest boxes for birds.
- Keep bird feeders topped up and continue to put food out on the ground and bird table.
- Keep the bird bath topped up and unfrozen for part of the day, if possible. Regardless of the cold, many birds still like to bathe.
- Regularly clean the bird bath and table, disposing of old food.
- Make sure the bird bath and table are kept clear of snow.
- Keep the pond from freezing over.
- Put out hedgehog food.

INSECTS
Butterflies, particularly brimstones and commas, can emerge during spells of sunshine. Now is the time to consider having a bee home. Homes for solitary bees (such as mason bees) are usually more successful than those for colony-forming bees. Bees usually colonise these homes in spring, hibernating in them over winter to emerge the following spring.

VARIED HABITATS
The best way to encourage wildlife into your garden is to provide a range of different habitats.
- **Ponds** Even the smallest pond will attract dragonflies, damselflies and other insects, as well as newts, toads and frogs. A pond also provides an important water source for all wildlife.
- **Logs** are a perfect habitat for insects as well as providing potential hibernation places for small mammals and amphibians and nesting sites for some birds. Retaining an old tree with cavities or splits in the trunk, or even just leaving a log or two in a corner, will benefit wildlife.
- **Hedges** provide important corridors for wildlife to move along safely, as well as protection from the elements, nesting and hibernation sites, and food. Trim hedges after the birds have eaten the berries (but before the nesting season begins). Replace a fence or exotic hedge with a native hedgerow of hawthorn (*Crataegus monogyna*), blackthorn (*Prunus spinosa*), field maple (*Acer campestre*) or hazel (*Corylus avellana*).
- **Compost heaps** Insects, which are an important food source, live in compost heaps.

FEBRUARY

Holiday, New Zealand (Waitangi Day)

Monday 8

Tuesday 9

Wednesday 10

New moon

Thursday 11

Chinese New Year

Friday 12

Saturday 13

Valentine's Day

Sunday 14

Barn owl *(Tyto alba)*

FEBRUARY

---

15 *Monday*

---

16 *Tuesday* Shrove Tuesday

---

17 *Wednesday* Ash Wednesday

---

18 *Thursday*

---

19 *Friday* First quarter

---

20 *Saturday*

---

21 *Sunday*

Blue tit *(Cyanistes caeruleus)*

FEBRUARY

Monday 22

Tuesday 23

Wednesday 24

Thursday 25

Friday 26

Full moon

Saturday 27

Sunday 28

Field mouse *(Apodemus sylvaticus)*

MARCH

1 *Monday* St David's Day

2 *Tuesday*

3 *Wednesday*

4 *Thursday*

5 *Friday*

6 *Saturday* Last quarter

7 *Sunday*

'Put out different types of bird food to attract particular species.'

BIRD FOOD AND FEEDERS
- Use wire mesh feeders for peanuts (but avoid putting these out until fledglings are old enough not to choke).
- Goldfinches love the tiny niger seed which needs a specially-designed feeder.
- Encourage ground-feeding birds such as robins and dunnocks by placing food on wire mesh positioned just off the ground.
- Place fat blocks in wire cages – plastic nets can be dangerous for some birds.
- Make your own fat blocks by melting suet into moulds such as coconut shells or logs with holes drilled into them.
- Clean feeders regularly and move them around the garden to avoid fouling the ground underneath.
- Water containers should be shallow, preferably with sloping sides and no more than 5cm (2in) deep.
- Put out different types of bird food to attract particular species.

JOBS FOR THE MONTH
- Put up nest boxes for birds and for bees.
- Top up bird feeders and put food out on the ground and bird table.
- Avoid chunky foods that might cause young fledglings to choke.
- Keep the bird bath topped up.
- Put out hedgehog food.
- Make your pond more wildlife friendly.
- Put out log, twig and rock piles to create shelter for wildlife.
- Sow or plant a wildflower meadow.

CHOOSING A BIRD TABLE
A bird table can be a simple tray, with or without a roof. A raised edge will retain food and a gap in each corner will allow water to drain away and facilitate cleaning. Avoid fancy designs that are difficult to clean. Choose a safe location, bearing in mind predators such as cats.

MARCH

Commonwealth Day

Monday 8

Tuesday 9

Wednesday 10

Thursday 11

Friday 12

New moon

Saturday 13

Mothering Sunday, UK and Republic of Ireland

Sunday 14

European goldfinch *(Carduelis carduelis)*

MARCH

---

15 *Monday*

---

16 *Tuesday*

---

17 *Wednesday*

St Patrick's Day
Holiday, Republic of Ireland
and Northern Ireland

---

18 *Thursday*

---

19 *Friday*

---

20 *Saturday*

Vernal Equinox (Spring begins)

---

21 *Sunday*

First quarter

Mullein caterpillar *(Cucullia verbasci)*

MARCH

Monday 22

Tuesday 23

Wednesday 24

Thursday 25

Friday 26

Saturday 27

Sunday 28

Full moon
Palm Sunday
First full day of Passover (Pesach)
British Summer Time begins

Red squirrel *(Sciurus vulgaris)*

29 *Monday*

30 *Tuesday*

31 *Wednesday*

1 *Thursday*   Maundy Thursday

2 *Friday*   Good Friday
                                                  Holiday, UK, Canada, Australia
                                                            and New Zealand

3 *Saturday*

4 *Sunday*   *Last quarter*
                                                                 Easter Sunday

Red fox *(Vulpes vulpes)*

'Plant annuals and perennials to encourage beneficial insects into the garden.'

JOBS FOR THE MONTH

- Put up nesting boxes for birds.
- Top up bird feeders and put food out on the ground and bird table.
- Avoid chunky foods that might cause young fledglings to choke.
- Keep the bird bath topped up.
- Put out hedgehog food.
- Make your pond more wildlife friendly.
- Create log, twig and rock piles to provide shelter for wildlife.
- Plant annuals and perennials (single flowers as opposed to double flowers) to encourage beneficial insects into the garden.

BATS

- Bats come out of hibernation and begin their breeding season. Nesting sites include in the eaves or behind weatherboarding on the south face of buildings. Most bat species eat midges and tiny insects.
- Make or buy a bat box and mount it on a sunny wall.

INSECTS

- Butterflies (such as brimstones, commas, tortoiseshells and cabbage whites) emerge as temperatures and sunshine increase.
- You may start to see bumble bees as the days become warmer.

BIRDS

- Migrant birds from Africa (such as willow warblers, house martins, swifts and swallows) have arrived.
- The nesting season is now well underway. The dawn chorus can be deafening as birds compete with each other for mates.

APRIL

Monday **5**

Easter Monday
Holiday, UK (exc. Scotland), Republic of Ireland,
Australia and New Zealand

Tuesday **6**

Wednesday **7**

Thursday **8**

Friday **9**

Saturday **10**

Sunday **11**

APRIL

---

12 *Monday*   New moon

---

13 *Tuesday*   First day of Ramadān (subject to sighting of the moon)

---

14 *Wednesday*

---

15 *Thursday*

---

16 *Friday*

---

17 *Saturday*

---

18 *Sunday*

Common noctule *(Nyctalus noctula)*

APRIL

Monday **19**

First quarter

Tuesday **20**

Birthday of Queen Elizabeth II

Wednesday **21**

Thursday **22**

St George's Day

Friday **23**

Saturday **24**

Anzac Day

Sunday **25**

Chaffinch *(Fringilla coelebs)*

APRIL & MAY

---

26 *Monday*

Holiday, Australia and New Zealand (Anzac Day)

---

27 *Tuesday*

Full moon

---

28 *Wednesday*

---

29 *Thursday*

---

30 *Friday*

---

1 *Saturday*

---

2 *Sunday*

'Avoid disturbing nest boxes in garden shrubs and hedges.'

JOBS FOR THE MONTH
- Put up nest boxes.
- Avoid disturbing nest boxes in garden shrubs and hedges.
- Top up bird feeders and put food out on the ground and bird table. Avoid chunky foods that might cause young fledglings to choke.
- Regularly top up and clean out your bird bath and table.
- Make your pond more wildlife friendly.
- Remove weeds from ponds, leaving them on the side for twenty-four hours to allow trapped creatures to return to the water before adding them to the compost heap.
- Create log, twig and rock piles to create shelter for wildlife.
- Choose annuals and perennials to attract insects.
- Leave informal hedges untrimmed for a while to provide food and shelter for wildlife.

CHOOSING BIRD FOOD
If you want to see more of a particular species in your garden, try leaving out food particular to their requirements.
- **Dunnocks** crumbs of bread, fat, and small seeds on the ground
- **Finches** berry cakes
- **Goldfinches** niger seeds
- **Robins** live mealworms
- **Sparrows, finches and nuthatches** sunflower heads
- **Starlings** peanut cakes
- **Tits** insect cakes
- **Thrushes and blackbirds** fruit such as over-ripe apples, raisins and songbird mix scattered on the ground.

MAKE A FAT BALL
Bird food doesn't need to be expensive and you can easily make your own fat balls.
1. Mix together one part fat (suet or lard work well) to two parts seed, transfer to a saucepan and gently heat, stirring until the fat melts.
2. To make fat balls, mould the seed mixture into balls using your hands. Space apart on a tray and place in the fridge to set for 24 hours.
3. Once the fat balls are solid, put out in the garden in a regular bird feeder or fat ball feeder.

MAY

Last quarter
Early Spring Bank Holiday, UK
Holiday, Republic of Ireland

Monday 3

Tuesday 4

Wednesday 5

Thursday 6

Friday 7

Saturday 8

Mother's Day, USA, Canada,
Australia and New Zealand

Sunday 9

Honey bee *(Apis mellifera)*

MAY

---

10 *Monday*

---

11 *Tuesday*

New moon

---

12 *Wednesday*

Eid al-Fitr (end of Ramadân)
(subject to sighting of the moon)

---

13 *Thursday*

Ascension Day

---

14 *Friday*

---

15 *Saturday*

---

16 *Sunday*

Common frog *(Rana temporaria)*

MAY

Feast of Weeks (Shavuot) begins

Monday **17**

Tuesday **18**

First quarter

Wednesday **19**

Thursday **20**

Friday **21**

Saturday **22**

Whit Sunday

Sunday **23**

Common kingfisher *(Alcedo atthis)*

MAY

24 *Monday*

25 *Tuesday*

26 *Wednesday*

Full moon

27 *Thursday*

28 *Friday*

29 *Saturday*

30 *Sunday*

Trinity Sunday

Campanula flowers covering brick steps in an English garden

'Encourage amphibians into your garden by creating a pond or other body of water.'

JOBS FOR THE MONTH

- Continue to put out food for birds on a regular basis.
- Consider adding a bird bath as it can be a vital source of drinking water for birds; birds also like to bathe all year. Always clean it regularly and keep it topped up.
- Build a ladybird 'hotel' using bundles of hollow stems or twigs.
- Put up a bat nesting box.
- Put out hedgehog food.
- Thin out, cut back or divide excessive new growth on aquatic plants.
- Create log, twig and rock piles to provide shelter for small mammals and insects.
- Use wildlife-friendly slug pellets.
- Mow spring flowering meadows once bulb foliage has died down.
- Plant nectar-heavy plants in sheltered areas to encourage bees and butterflies.

IN THE GARDEN

Avoid pruning hip-producing roses – the hips are a useful source of food for wildlife.

MAMMALS AND AMPHIBIANS

Hedgehog litters are being born. You may see or hear their parents foraging for food at night. Tadpoles are developing their hind legs and are emerging from the water to seek shelter among marginal pond plants; they are now very vulnerable to predators.

PONDS AND WILDLIFE

- Encourage amphibians into your garden by creating a pond or other body of water.
- Frogs and toads need a space above water on which to rest and breathe. A few well-placed rocks or logs will provide this if there is no shallow water.
- To encourage newts introduce non-invasive submerged aquatic plants. Newts lay their eggs on narrow-leaved water plants.
- Amphibians hibernate in the autumn and look for shelter in log piles, hedge bottoms, compost heaps and under stones, as well as at the bottom of ponds.
- Allow new ponds to colonise naturally, as transferring spawn or tadpoles from elsewhere could introduce disease.
- Remove blanket weed from your pond to allow other plants and fish room to grow.

MAY & JUNE

Spring Bank Holiday, UK

Monday 31

Tuesday 1

Wednesday 2

Corpus Christi

Thursday 3

Friday 4

Saturday 5

Sunday 6

JUNE

---

7 *Monday*

Holiday, Republic of Ireland
Holiday, New Zealand (The Queen's Birthday)

---

8 *Tuesday*

---

9 *Wednesday*

---

10 *Thursday*

New moon

---

11 *Friday*

---

12 *Saturday*

The Queen's Official Birthday (subject to confirmation)

---

13 *Sunday*

Bumblebee *(Bombus hortorum)*

JUNE

Holiday, Australia (The Queen's Birthday)

Monday 14

Tuesday 15

Wednesday 16

Thursday 17

First quarter

Friday 18

Saturday 19

Father's Day, UK, Republic of Ireland, USA and Canada

Sunday 20

Nuthatch *(Sitta europaea)*

JUNE

---

21 *Monday*   Summer Solstice (Summer begins)

---

22 *Tuesday*

---

23 *Wednesday*

---

24 *Thursday*   Full moon

---

25 *Friday*

---

26 *Saturday*

---

27 *Sunday*

Common hawker *(Aeshna juncea)*

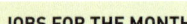

JOBS FOR THE MONTH
- Top up bird feeders and put food out on the ground and bird tables.
- Avoid chunky foods that might cause fledglings to choke.
- Keep the bird bath topped up and clean regularly.
- Plant marigolds around the vegetable patch to attract hoverflies, which prey on pests.
- Plant annuals and perennials to attract insects.
- Trim hedges less often to allow wildlife to shelter and feed in them.
- Leave nesting birds undisturbed in garden shrubs and trees.
- Avoid deadheading roses that produce hips, as these are a valuable food source.
- Top up ponds and water features if necessary. Aerating the water using a hose with spray attachment adds oxygen, which will help the fish.
- Remove dead foliage and blooms from aquatic plants.

INSECTS
Harmless hoverflies are in abundance. They are good garden pest catchers, along with wasps which eat flies and grubs; they are also useful flower pollinators.

'Wasps eat flies and grubs; they are also useful flower pollinators.'

SPIDERS
- Spiders have an important role to play in the garden. As well as eating insects, they are part of the food chain and are a food source for birds.
- Plant tall plants and dense bushes to create scaffolding for spiders to build their webs on.
- Cover bare soil with mulch. This keeps it moist and provides a home for insects, a food source for spiders.

BATS
- Compost heaps and ponds will produce the type of insects bats like to eat.
- Grow plants with flowers that are likely to attract moths and other night-flying insects. White or pale-coloured flowers are more likely to be seen by such species.
- Be insect tolerant. Spare a few caterpillars to feed a bat.
- Avoid using pesticides where possible.

JUNE & JULY

Monday 28

Tuesday 29

Wednesday 30

Last quarter
Holiday, Canada (Canada Day)

Thursday 1

Friday 2

Saturday 3

Independence Day

Sunday 4

JULY

5 *Monday* Holiday, USA (Independence Day)

6 *Tuesday*

7 *Wednesday*

8 *Thursday*

9 *Friday*

10 *Saturday* New moon

11 *Sunday*

Wild rabbit *(Oryctolagus cuniculus)*

JULY

Battle of the Boyne
Holiday, Northern Ireland

Monday **12**

Tuesday **13**

Wednesday **14**

St Swithin's Day

Thursday **15**

Friday **16**

First quarter

Saturday **17**

Sunday **18**

Seven-spot ladybird *(Coccinella septempunctata)*

JULY

19 *Monday*

20 *Tuesday*

21 *Wednesday*

22 *Thursday*

23 *Friday*

24 *Saturday*   *Full moon*

25 *Sunday*

Common starling *(Sturnus vulgaris)*

JULY & AUGUST

Monday 26

Tuesday 27

Wednesday 28

Thursday 29

Friday 30

Last quarter

Saturday 31

Sunday 1

Painted lady *(Vanessa cardui)*

AUGUST

2 *Monday*

3 *Tuesday*

4 *Wednesday*

5 *Thursday*

6 *Friday*

7 *Saturday*

8 *Sunday* *New moon*

BIRDS

- Many birds are fairly secretive in late summer, hiding away while their feathers change during the summer moult.
- Birdsong is much reduced during this month. New young birds can be seen exploring their environment. In hot, dry weather, many birds enjoy 'dust-bathing' as well as washing in the bird bath.

'In hot, dry weather many birds enjoy 'dust-bathing' as well as washing in the bird bath.'

JOBS FOR THE MONTH

- Top up bird feeders and put food out on the ground and bird tables.
- Avoid chunky foods that might cause young fledglings to choke.
- Keep the bird bath topped up.
- Clean bird baths and tables regularly.
- Plant marigolds around the vegetable patch to attract hoverflies for pest control.
- Dead-head flowers to encourage them to produce more blooms and pollen for insects.
- Put out hedgehog food.
- Plant annuals and perennials to attract insects.
- Trim hedges less frequently to allow wildlife to shelter and feed in them.
- Leave nesting birds undisturbed in garden shrubs and trees.
- Allow seed heads to develop on some plants as a food source.

MAMMALS AND AMPHIBIANS

Young frogs and newts start to leave the ponds where they were born to move further afield.

ENCOURAGE MOTHS

- Plant sea lavender, buddleia, *Centranthus ruber* and *Lychnis* to attract day-flying moths.
- Plant night-flowering, nectar-rich plants.
- Leave longer grasses, thistles and knapweeds in the garden.
- Oak, birch, willow, hawthorn and hornbeam support moth caterpillars, as do many ornamental garden plants.

AUGUST

Monday 9

Islamic New Year

Tuesday 10

Wednesday 11

Thursday 12

Friday 13

Saturday 14

First quarter

Sunday 15

Colourful wildflowers

AUGUST

16 *Monday*

17 *Tuesday*

18 *Wednesday*

19 *Thursday*

20 *Friday*

21 *Saturday*

22 *Sunday*

Full moon

Common newt *(Lissotriton vulgaris)*

AUGUST

Monday 23

Tuesday 24

Wednesday 25

Thursday 26

Friday 27

Saturday 28

Sunday 29

Yellow-clubbed hoverfly *(Scaeva selenitica)*

30 *Monday*
Last quarter
Summer Bank Holiday, UK (exc. Scotland)

31 *Tuesday*

1 *Wednesday*

2 *Thursday*

3 *Friday*

4 *Saturday*

5 *Sunday*
Father's Day, Australia and New Zealand

JOBS FOR THE MONTH

- Continue to feed birds, avoiding chunky foods that might cause fledglings to choke.
- Keep the bird bath topped up and clean it regularly.
- Put out hedgehog food and construct a hedgehog hibernation box.
- Trim hedges less frequently to create shelter for wildlife. They can also be an important food source.
- Give meadows a final cut before winter.
- Cover the pond surface with netting before leaf fall gets underway.

PREPARE FOR WINTER

Help hibernating creatures survive the cold weather by making hibernation places in your garden such as creating a log pile for beetles, making a 'ladybird hotel' out of hollow stems and building a hedgehog box. Even a pile of old leaves left undisturbed will provide a home for small mammals and many insects.

IN THE GARDEN

- Leave meadow clippings to lie for a couple of days before removing to allow wildlife to crawl back into the grass.
- Autumn daisies are important for butterflies and bees as there are fewer other plants in flower for them to feed on. Many butterflies (such as peacock, small tortoiseshell, and speckled wood) are still about.
- The evening is the best time to spot mammals, and if it is warm, this is a good opportunity for bat watching.

'The evening is the best time to spot mammals.'

SEPTEMBER

Holiday, USA (Labor Day)
Holiday, Canada (Labour Day)

Monday 6

New moon
Jewish New Year (Rosh Hashanah)

Tuesday 7

Wednesday 8

Thursday 9

Friday 10

Saturday 11

Sunday 12

Lesser redpoll *(Acanthis cabaret)*

SEPTEMBER

13 *Monday* *First quarter*

14 *Tuesday*

15 *Wednesday*

16 *Thursday* Day of Atonement (Yom Kippur)

17 *Friday*

18 *Saturday*

19 *Sunday*

European mole *(Talpa europaea)*

SEPTEMBER

Monday 20

Full moon
First day of Tabernacles (Sukkot)

Tuesday 21

Autumnal Equinox (Autumn begins)

Wednesday 22

Thursday 23

Friday 24

Saturday 25

Sunday 26

Great spotted woodpecker *(Dendrocopos major)*

27 *Monday*

---

28 *Tuesday*

---

29 *Wednesday*

Last quarter
Michaelmas Day

---

30 *Thursday*

---

1 *Friday*

---

2 *Saturday*

---

3 *Sunday*

JOBS FOR THE MONTH

- Top up bird feeders and put food out on the ground and bird tables.
- All food, including peanuts, are safe as the breeding season is now over.
- Be careful when turning compost heaps, as frogs, toads and small animals may be sheltering there.
- Keep the bird bath topped up and clean regularly.
- Where possible leave seed heads standing to provide food and shelter for wildlife. If possible, leave mature ivy uncut to flower.
- Late flowering plants, such as Michaelmas daisies and agapanthus, provide nectar and pollen for the few winter insects.
- Make a leaf pile for hibernating mammals and overwintering ground-feeding birds; add in some logs to widen the appeal for a greater range of insects, or build a 'bug hotel'.

'Foxes may become nocturnal pests as food sources become scarce.'

MAMMALS

Foxes may become nocturnal pests as food sources become scarce, so always secure your rubbish. Other mammals start going into hibernation.

BIRDS

- Winter migrants start to arrive from colder, northern regions. Geese and ducks can be arriving in droves. In the garden you may spot finches, redwings and fieldfares.
- Starlings gather in large groups.

INSECTS

- Many butterflies, including tortoiseshell, are still about, along with hoverflies and ladybirds. Mature ivy flowers provide an excellent late nectar source for wildlife.
- Holly blue butterfly larvae can be seen as the little caterpillars feed on ivy. Although emerging caterpillars eat your plants they will grow into butterflies which help with pollination and look beautiful. The top favourite foods for caterpillars include stinging nettle, thistle, wild carrot, bird's foot trefoil, buckthorn and blackthorn.

OCTOBER

Monday 4

Tuesday 5

New moon

Wednesday 6

Thursday 7

Friday 8

Saturday 9

Sunday 10

Bloody-nosed beetle *(Timarcha tenebricosa)*

OCTOBER

---

11 *Monday*

---

12 *Tuesday*

---

13 *Wednesday*

First quarter

---

14 *Thursday*

---

15 *Friday*

---

16 *Saturday*

---

17 *Sunday*

House sparrow *(Passer domesticus)*

OCTOBER

Monday 18

Tuesday 19

Full moon

Wednesday 20

Thursday 21

Friday 22

Saturday 23

Sunday 24

Tawny owl *(Strix aluco)*

OCTOBER

25 *Monday*

Bank Holiday, Republic of Ireland
Holiday, New Zealand (Labour Day)

26 *Tuesday*

27 *Wednesday*

28 *Thursday*

Last quarter

29 *Friday*

30 *Saturday*

31 *Sunday*

Halloween
British Summer Time ends

A stone bird bath in an English country garden

JOBS FOR THE MONTH

- All bird food is now safe, so continue to put it out regularly.
- Keep the bird bath topped up and clean regularly.
- Make a hedgehog hibernation box (see Mammals, right).
- Leave seed heads standing to provide food and shelter for wildlife.
- Allow mature ivy to remain uncut for its flowers – the nectar is a food source for insects.
- Make a leaf pile for hibernating mammals and ground-feeding birds.
- Empty and clean out nest boxes with boiling water. When thoroughly dry, place a handful of wood shavings inside to provide winter shelter. It is illegal to remove unhatched eggs except between November and January.

'Check for hibernating toads or hedgehogs before lighting bonfires.'

MAMMALS

- Check for hibernating toads or hedgehogs before lighting bonfires.
- Make a hedgehog hibernation box using a sturdy upturned cardboard box, covered with plastic and then earth, stones and leaves (remembering to cut out an adequate entrance hole).
- Position the box in a quiet area, preferably against a bank, wall or fence. Make sure the entrance does not face north or north-east. The hedgehog will make its nest from garden debris.

POND CARE

- Regularly shake off leaves from protective nets over ponds. Rake out the leaves that are not netted.
- Conserve water and connect your water butt so that it fills the pond automatically during heavy rain.
- Encourage newts to breed by introducing some non-invasive submerged aquatic plants into the pond. Newts lay their eggs on narrow-leaved plants.
- Create a nearby log pile using the biggest logs you can find. All kinds of insects will love it.

NOVEMBER

All Saints' Day

Monday 1

Tuesday 2

Wednesday 3

New moon

Thursday 4

Guy Fawkes Night

Friday 5

Saturday 6

Sunday 7

NOVEMBER

8 *Monday*

9 *Tuesday*

10 *Wednesday*

11 *Thursday*

First quarter
Holiday, USA (Veterans Day)
Holiday, Canada (Remembrance Day)

12 *Friday*

13 *Saturday*

14 *Sunday*

Remembrance Sunday

European badger *(Meles meles)*

NOVEMBER

Monday **15**

Tuesday **16**

Wednesday **17**

Thursday **18**

Full moon

Friday **19**

Saturday **20**

Sunday **21**

urasian wren *(Troglodytes troglodytes)*

NOVEMBER

22 *Monday*

23 *Tuesday*

24 *Wednesday*

25 *Thursday*   Holiday, USA (Thanksgiving)

26 *Friday*

27 *Saturday*   Last quarter

28 *Sunday*   First Sunday in Advent
                                                             Hannukah begins (at sunset)

Angle shades moth (*Phlogophora meticulosa*)

JOBS FOR THE MONTH

- Top up bird feeders and put food out on the ground and bird tables. Once a feeding regime is established try to keep to it, as this will encourage birds to return.
- All bird food, including peanuts, is safe, as the breeding season is over.
- Keep the bird bath topped up and ice-free.
- Clean bird baths and tables regularly.
- Where possible leave seed heads standing to provide food and shelter for wildlife.
- If possible, leave mature ivy uncut to flower.
- Make a leaf pile for hibernating mammals and wintering ground-feeding birds.

CHRISTMAS DECORATIONS

Holly (*Ilex*) is a traditional part of Christmas. However, holly berries are a valuable source of food for birds so think twice before depriving them.

'Once a feeding regime is established try to keep to it, as this will encourage birds to return.'

BIRDS

- Now is the time to make sure you are including fat in food you put out for birds.
- Make sure any fat blocks are in wire cages and not plastic nets, which can be harmful.
- Wrens and other small birds appreciate finely chopped bacon rind and grated cheese.
- Put out food regularly so birds don't waste vital energy on visiting when there is no food.
- Add an open-fronted nest box to your garden to encourage robins to nest.

NOVEMBER & DECEMBER

Monday 29

St Andrew's Day

Tuesday 30

Wednesday 1

Thursday 2

Friday 3

New moon

Saturday 4

Sunday 5

DECEMBER

6 *Monday* Hannukah ends

7 *Tuesday*

8 *Wednesday*

9 *Thursday*

10 *Friday*

11 *Saturday* First quarter

12 *Sunday*

Frosted berries on a rowan tree

DECEMBER

Monday 13

Tuesday 14

Wednesday 15

Thursday 16

Friday 17

Saturday 18

Full moon

Sunday 19

Coal tit (*Periparus ater*)

DECEMBER

20 *Monday*

21 *Tuesday*

Winter Solstice (Winter begins)

22 *Wednesday*

23 *Thursday*

24 *Friday*

Christmas Eve

25 *Saturday*

Christmas Day

26 *Sunday*

Boxing Day (St Stephen's Day)

Bird table hanging from a branch

DECEMBER & JANUARY 2022

Monday 27

Last quarter
Holiday, UK, Republic of Ireland, USA,
Canada, Australia and New Zealand (Christmas Day)

Tuesday 28

Holiday, UK, Republic of Ireland, USA,
Canada, Australia and New Zealand (Boxing Day)

Wednesday 29

Thursday 30

Friday 31

New Year's Eve

Saturday 1

New Year's Day

Sunday 2

Robin *(Erithacus rubecula)*

YEAR PLANNER

JANUARY	JULY
FEBRUARY	AUGUST
MARCH	SEPTEMBER
APRIL	OCTOBER
MAY	NOVEMBER
JUNE	DECEMBER